DISINFORMATION

DISINFORMATION

The RISE of FALSE NARRATIVES

Matt Doeden

LERNER PUBLICATIONS ◆ MINNEAPOLIS

Lerner Publications Company
An imprint of Lerner Publishing Group, Inc.
241 First Avenue North
Minneapolis, MN 55401 USA

For reading levels and more information, look up this title at www.lernerbooks.com.

Main body text set in ITC Garamond Std Book.
Typeface provided by Adobe Systems.

Editor: Nicole Berglund **Designer:** Athena Currier **Photo Editor:** Cynthia Zemlicka

Library of Congress Cataloging-in-Publication Data

Names: Doeden, Matt, author.
Title: Disinformation : the rise of false narratives / Matt Doeden.
Description: Minneapolis : Lerner Publications, [2026] | Series: Gateway headlines | Includes bibliographical references and index. | Audience: Ages 9–14 | Audience: Grades 4–6 | Summary: "Disinformation is false information that is spread on purpose. It might be created as a joke or to harm others. Readers explore the history of disinformation, from communities in the 1400s to global news in the 2020s"— Provided by publisher.
Identifiers: LCCN 2024038598 (print) | LCCN 2024038599 (ebook) | ISBN 9798765684160 (paperback) | ISBN 9798765669419 (library binding) | ISBN 9798765677698 (epub)
Subjects: LCSH: Disinformation—Juvenile literature. | Disinformation—History—Juvenile literature.
Classification: LCC HM1231 .D64 2026 (print) | LCC HM1231 (ebook) | DDC 001.9—dc23/eng/20241121

LC record available at https://lccn.loc.gov/2024038598
LC ebook record available at https://lccn.loc.gov/2024038599

Manufactured in the United States of America
1-1011883-53912-12/5/2024

Table of Contents

In March 2017 what appeared to be a shocking news story went viral across social media. The article's author claimed that the popular candy Reese's Peanut Butter Cups contained several toxic ingredients. The article stated that the toxic ingredients in the candy could cause everything from cancer to attention deficit hyperactivity disorder (ADHD). According to the author, the dangerous candy was about to be removed from store shelves worldwide and people should stop eating it right away.

Some parents panicked, and some kids struggled to understand why eating their favorite candy was suddenly a terrible health risk. The Reese's Peanut Butter Cups article spread as alarmed readers continued to share and repost it. The article became clickbait for a handful of nonmainstream news sites. These sites are smaller and less reliable than mainstream news sites, such as the *New York Times* or ABC News. Clickbait is a sensational headline, article, story, or image whose purpose is to get as many clicks as possible. The truth or factual accuracy of the story did not matter to the owners of these news sites. All that mattered was that the article got people clicking onto their sites to generate more ad revenue. Once the story took off, it was almost impossible to stop it.

Ad revenue is money made from ads displayed on TV, radio, websites, and other media.

But the story was fake. Reese's Peanut Butter Cups were not a healthful food, but they were no less healthful than most other candy. Reese's Peanut Butter Cups had become a victim of internet disinformation, the intentional spread of fake news.

It was easy to understand why. The fake news article preyed on readers' fears. It was written in a way that sounded very scientific, but the science was incorrect. The website Snopes follows and fact-checks these sorts of viral news stories. According to Snopes, "Ultimately, the claims presented in [the article] rely on outdated, irrelevant, or factually incomplete information."

Most people recognized that the post was disinformation. But some people fell for it and never followed up on the story in the days and weeks that followed. They went on believing that eating the peanut butter cups would put their health at risk. So the article's lie lived on.

It is a familiar story in the age of the internet and social media. News can take on a life of its own, spreading rapidly even when it's untrue. And with the dawn of new technology, the age of disinformation may be just beginning.

Disinformation in History

There are multiple kinds of bad information. *Misinformation* is untrue news caused by a mistake. A reporter might not understand what they are reporting, or they may report facts that came from an unreliable source. Although the story or facts are untrue, the reporter did not intentionally share untrue news.

Disinformation is lying and misleading on purpose. People may share disinformation because they are attacking an opposing position. They could just be playing a joke. No matter the reason, the whole point of disinformation is to confuse people and hide the truth. Disinformation may thrive online, but it's not new. It has existed throughout human history. The spreading of false information really took off after German inventor Johannes Gutenberg introduced the printing press in Europe in the mid-1400s. The invention allowed people to print and distribute information on a massive scale—for good and for bad.

The results could be tragic. In Trent, Italy, in 1475, a young Christian boy named Simonino was found dead. A false story spread that the Jewish community there had captured and killed him. Many people believed the disinformation. They rounded up innocent Jewish people. The Catholic Church in Italy realized that it was a fake story. The church tried to stop what was happening, but it was too late. Fifteen Jewish people were found guilty and killed.

Over the following centuries, fake news continued to thrive. Some of it was mostly harmless, such as stories of sea monsters and miracles. An 1835 story convinced people that scientists had discovered an alien civilization on the moon. But other disinformation was far more

Trent, Italy

harmful. It focused on racism and hateful religious stances. Its goal was often to spark violence.

By the early 1900s, many newspapers were rejecting careless and unprofessional reporting. Reporters and editors fact-checked their stories before publishing. Of course, it wasn't the end of disinformation. But people seeking objective, or unbiased, and responsible reporting finally had better places to turn to for their news.

Still, the truth could be hard to find. People spread

disinformation to trick others. In the 1930s many people grew interested in the Loch Ness Monster. People flocked to Loch Ness, a lake in Scotland, to search for the giant beast. Everyone wanted to be the first to snap a picture to prove that it existed.

In 1934 it seemed to have finally happened. Colonel Robert Wilson captured an image that showed something in the water. Wilson claimed that the photo showed the monster. The image ended up on newspapers around the globe. For many, Wilson's

Colonel Robert Wilson's 1934 photo that he claimed showed the Loch Ness Monster

photo was the proof they'd been seeking. The Loch Ness Monster was real! Decades later, the truth came out. The photo was a hoax—a trick. What appeared to be a monster in Wilson's photo had been built out of a toy submarine, then held close to the camera to appear large.

With the outbreaks of World War I (1914–1918) and World War II (1939–1945), a type of news called propaganda boomed. Propaganda was news designed to promote a stance, such as patriotism, or to create fear or hatred of an enemy. It was often exaggerated or completely untrue. During World War II, German newspapers printed cartoons showing white Germans as superior to other people. Meanwhile, the United States fed false information to Japanese people to make them believe the war was going more poorly for Japan than it was. The hope was that the disinformation would crush the spirit of the Japanese people and cause them to stop supporting the war.

A Nazi propoganda poster from World War II

YELLOW JOURNALISM

In the late 1800s, newspapers were big businesses. Papers competed with one another for readers. This led some to post the most amazing articles they could. It was a practice called yellow journalism. The truth of a story didn't matter much. What mattered was how alarming and attention-grabbing the headline was.

In 1898 an explosion rocked a US battleship in Cuba called the USS *Maine* (*below*). The ship sank. Newspapers quickly labeled it an attack from Spain. No evidence supported that claim, but the tension it caused helped lead to the Spanish-American War of 1898 later that year.

The Early Internet

Computer networks date back to the 1950s. But early networks and computers were slow and clunky. They weren't built to move large amounts of data. Most computers lacked a standard way to talk to one another, and they couldn't link up.

College students use desktop computers in the 1980s.

In 1983 a new way for computers to connect to one another was introduced. This large network of computers became known as the internet. At the time, this wasn't big news, and it wasn't a groundbreaking, life-changing technology for most people. Almost all of the people who used it were researchers and computer developers. For about a decade, most of the world carried on with no idea of what the internet did, and many didn't even know that the internet existed.

The internet slowly grew. In 1991 a system called the World Wide Web started. The web boomed throughout the rest of the 1990s, opening the internet up to new people. For the first time, the internet became part of a global culture. It offered ways to learn and communicate that many people had never before imagined.

Suddenly, anyone with an internet connection had access to a wealth of information. They could turn to the web for instant news or weather, rather than waiting for a TV broadcast or the next day's newspaper. But very early on, the idea that anyone could put anything online was a worry. Terry Pratchett, an author and journalist, saw the internet as a place where lies could thrive. In a 1995 interview with Microsoft founder Bill Gates, Pratchett said, "It's all there: there's no way of finding out whether this stuff has any [truth] to it or whether someone just made it up."

Pratchett and other people were right about disinformation online. No one was in charge of the internet, and people could make any claims online. Rumors spread and fake stories were easy to create and publish. In 1996 a professor at Minnesota State University, Mankato put up a fake site about the city of Mankato. It told of ancient pyramids and whale watching along the Minnesota River. All of it was untrue. The professor used the site to teach students that they couldn't believe everything on the internet. But not everyone was in on the joke. Two people found the site and booked vacations to Mankato.

Bill Gates uses the computer program Microsoft 95 in 1995.

Meanwhile, criminals took to the web to scam victims out of their money. They created fake sites to trick people into giving bank details. They also created online stores. The criminals collected money from purchases without sending goods to the buyers. More and more, people were becoming aware that much of what was online was not reliable.

The Rise of Social Media

In the early days of the internet, creating fake news on the web required people to set up a website. But in the early 2000s, social media became a new way to spread news. Social media sites allow users to post their own stories, updates, images, and links. In 2004 the site Myspace became the first social media site to have more than one million users. People could post updates to their Myspace pages for their friends and followers to see.

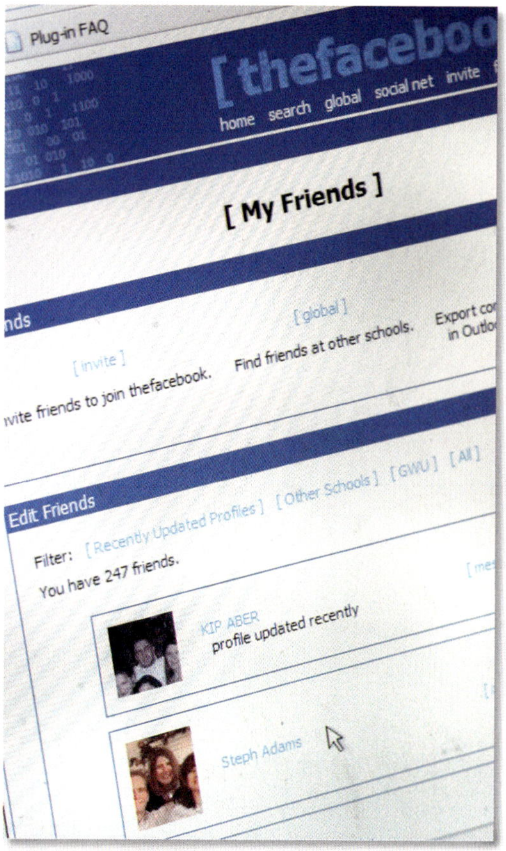

The Facebook was created in 2004 by four college students, including Mark Zuckerberg, and the name was later changed to Facebook.

By 2010 Facebook was the most popular social media platform with more than half a billion users. That number grew to more than one billion by 2016. For most people, Facebook was a way to keep up with friends and family. Other people saw it as a way of spreading news—both real and fake.

In 2012 Hurricane Sandy hit the East Coast of the United States. Fake

New Jersey is hit by Hurricane Sandy in 2012.

news stories about the natural disaster poured in. One article falsely said that the New York Stock Exchange was flooded, while other articles showed fake images of sharks swimming through flooded city streets. At a time when people wanted real news about the dangerous situation, fake stories made it hard to know what was really happening.

Most major news organizations try to present news that is true, factual, and accurate. They also present news that looks at all sides of a story. But many people on social media use it to spread news that promotes their own perspective or idea—or to make an opposing stance look bad.

Some people are willing to bend the truth or to lie to send the message they want. In 2017 Native American peoples were protesting the building of an oil pipeline that would run from North Dakota to Illinois. A social media story reported that police were burning the Native Americans' tipis and violently cracking down on peaceful protesters. The story came with a heartbreaking image of the burning tipis. But it was fake. It never happened.

A crowd protests at the White House against the building of the Dakota Access Pipeline in 2017.

The photos were from the 2007 movie *Bury My Heart at Wounded Knee*. That didn't stop countless people from posting and sharing the disinformation.

That same year a viral video showed a Muslim girl in Florida being beaten up in a fight. The girl's father later claimed that the assault had come because of the girl's religion. Many shared the video as an example of racism. After their investigation, police discovered that the fight had nothing to do with race or religion. The fight was over a romantic relationship—although many people never learned the truth of it. Racism against historically marginalized groups is a significant problem, but these stories were fake. These examples show how a powerful image or video can shape a person's opinion even when the context is missing or distorted.

ECHO CHAMBER

Social media sites such as Facebook track the sorts of stories that users click on and share. Then the sites feed users more stories—both real and fake—that match a similar theme. This can create an echo chamber. In echo chambers, people are only exposed to opinions they agree with. They never see the other side of an argument. Echo chambers can cause people to become inflexible in their thinking and less tolerant of opposing viewpoints.

Weaponizing the News

Social media and the internet have changed how people learn about political issues and how they form opinions. Candidates and political groups work to put out real news to support themselves and their positions. Some of them also share stories about themselves or their opponents that are false or only partly true to rally their supporters. Some candidates label any story that casts them in a bad light as fake news—even if it's true.

In 2016 a story hit the news that US presidential candidate Hillary Clinton was using a pizza shop in Washington, DC, to abuse children. People were outraged, and one man even went to the pizza shop

Hillary Clinton speaks at a rally a few months before the 2016 US presidential election.

with a gun to investigate. The story was false, and it was quickly debunked. But it had real-world consequences. The man who brought the gun was arrested, and some people kept believing the story up to and after the election that Clinton lost.

That was one example among many fake political news stories. Much of the fake news surrounding the 2016 US election came from Russian groups. They spread one false story after another to create confusion and fighting among Americans. The disinformation became such a concern that Facebook and other social media sites had to change their rules about what was offered as news content.

Things got even worse four years later. The 2020 US presidential race between Joe Biden and Donald Trump

Joe Biden (right) speaks in October 2020 at the final 2020 US presidential debate.

was filled with disinformation. It got even nastier after the election was over. Biden won in a very close race. Trump refused to accept defeat. He insisted that Biden's victory had been rigged—and some of his supporters believed it. "The fact is we won the presidential election, we won it big," he said at a rally after the election.

Trump and his supporters created stories about rigged voting machines and cheating by election officials. The fake news took off on social media. No proof existed that anything had been rigged or stolen, but once the idea was out there, there was no stopping it. People who were angry over the election results were ready to believe that Trump had been cheated.

Some of Trump's supporters were outraged. On January 6, 2021, they stormed the US Capitol in Washington, DC. Their goal was to overturn the result of the election. Many of them believed that their attack would cause Trump to remain in office. The mob broke into the Capitol and raided offices. They made threats to hurt politicians with whom they disagreed. One person was shot and killed in the attack. Several others, including police officers, died soon after. The attack all happened because of disinformation.

"There is truth and there are lies," said President Biden in his inauguration speech shortly after the attack. "Lies told for power and for profit. And each of us has a duty and responsibility, as citizens, as Americans, and especially as leaders . . . to defend the truth and to defeat the lies."

Trump supporters storm the US Capitol on January 6, 2021.

The problem of fake news is not limited to the United States or to elections. War broke out between Israel and the terrorist group Hamas in 2023. The fighting on the ground was real, but the reports about the war often were not. One story reported that US Marines had joined in the fight. It showed a picture of the marines arriving. The report was untrue, and the picture actually showed marines arriving in Romania in 2022. Another story said that a black flag being flown over a mosque was a call to war for all Muslims. That was also a lie. The black flag was a sign of mourning for those killed in the fighting. The constant stream of lies made it hard for people to know what was really happening. With so much fake news, people became skeptical even of the real news.

US officials have seen the danger that disinformation can cause. In 2023 Senator Amy Klobuchar (D-MN) and Representative Yvette Clarke (D-NY) introduced a bill called the REAL Political Advertisements Act. If passed, the law would force political ads to clearly state when any of their content was created by artificial intelligence (AI). Artificial intelligence is technology that seems to mimic human intelligence. It can operate computer programs or generate content such as images or text.

Senator Amy Klobuchar speaks to the press at the US Capitol in 2023.

CREATING VOTES

A 2024 story accused President Biden of flying more than three hundred thousand illegal immigrants from Latin America to the United States. The article said that Biden wanted to use them to cheat in the election. The story spread rapidly, especially among supporters of Biden's opponent, Donald Trump.
It was a lie. Nobody had any evidence to support the article, but that made little difference to many people who wanted to believe anything that was bad about an opposing political candidate.

Science and Disinformation

News articles that deal with science can be a major source of bad information. Sometimes, it's misinformation. Usually, reporters aren't scientists. They try to explain research or scientific observations in a way readers can easily understand. But sometimes, that means that they overlook important details, or they make things sound simpler than they really are.

In 2020 COVID-19 was sweeping across the globe. The new disease struck fear in people. They turned to the internet for news on what was happening and to learn how to protect themselves. Much of the reporting was good and helpful. But other stories contained false information.

States began announcing COVID-19 lockdowns in March 2020.

One popular story claimed that high doses of vitamin C could cure COVID-19. It seemed like a reasonable idea. After all, vitamin C is important for a healthy immune system. But the story was not backed by any scientific research. No study had shown that the vitamin could cure, or even prevent, the disease. It gave people a false sense of safety.

"Vitamin C does have some small effect on the common cold," explained Peter McCaffery, a biochemistry professor at the University of Aberdeen. "[But] it's unlikely that taking large amounts of vitamin C supplements will cure a COVID-19 infection—or have a large effect at all."

Sometimes, people try to make fake articles look real and scientific. It's disinformation. A 2014 article claimed that solar panels were draining the sun of its energy. The author warned that using this renewable energy source was putting our star at risk of dying out. The official-looking article referred to imaginary scientific studies to prove it. The article itself was written as satire—a style of writing that makes fun of a person or position. But not everyone understood that the article was satire. Some alarmed readers believed the article's claim that solar panels could wipe out the sun.

Solar panels were again targeted by disinformation in 2021. Authors wrote that solar panels were actually heating the globe. Building more solar panels, they said, could cause everything from bigger storms to droughts in the Amazon rainforest. Much of the data the authors used was real, but they drew conclusions that science didn't support. The disinformation was a scare tactic.

Many people use fake news to deny climate change, while other people use it to support climate change. In 2023 an image of flowers blooming in Antarctica went viral. The image of bright blooming flowers showed a large iceberg floating in the background. People took it as proof that climate change was causing the poles to melt and also turn green. But the picture wasn't from Antarctica. It was from Greenland, where such blooms are normal and seasonal. The point of the story was to cause confusion and distrust.

This viral photo of Greenland used as disinformation was first posted on Twitter, now X.

PSEUDOSCIENCE

Real, well-researched science is a key to understanding some of the world's problems. Scientists work hard to identify problems, their causes, and possible solutions. But just because an article sounds scientific doesn't make it true. Many people use pseudoscience to back false claims. Pseudoscience looks and sounds scientific. Although it mentions studies and provides data, it's not actually scientific. The data is often faked or taken out of context. By making it look official and scientific, authors hope to confuse people who don't know any better.

Spotting Disinformation

Let's say you're online. Maybe an alarming headline pops up in your news feed or a friend or relative posts something attention-grabbing to social media. You can't resist, so you click. The news is sensational. It goes against everything you thought you knew about a person or an issue. Maybe it seems mean or hateful. Is it real, or is it disinformation? How can you tell the difference?

First consider the source. Does it come from a long-standing news site with a good reputation, or is it from a social media post or a site that you've never

Doing research can help avoid the spread of disinformation.

heard of before? A site you've never heard of may not be trustworthy. When you click on the article or social media post, are you met with a wall of advertisements and pop-ups? If so, the article might be clickbait.

Even if an article comes from a less well-known source, that doesn't automatically make it bad. Many smaller sites do good, honest reporting and cover stories that major news outlets might overlook. But if news comes from a little-known source, it can be a sign that you shouldn't take the article at face value. You might need to do a bit more research to verify if the claims are true.

Pay close attention to how the article is written. Does it seem as if a professional writer wrote it? Is it well-written with proper grammar, punctuation, and structure? If the writing is sloppy, that could be a red flag. Most professional news outlets have trained writers and editors to make sure the writing is clear and properly written. If it's filled with grammar and spelling errors, your confidence in it should be low.

Next, look carefully at the content of the article. Is it realistic, or are the claims just too amazing or shocking to be true? Is it objective? Does the writer make an effort to cover both sides of the issue, or do they show a bias—favoring one side? Opinion-based articles are common. They serve an important purpose in media to discuss issues. But for facts about an issue, always look for objectively written news, not opinions.

Scientific articles should be even more objective because they must be reviewed before being published. Does the article seem one-sided and written to alarm, frighten, or anger the reader? After reading the article, check the author's sources. Do they cite real scientific studies?

If you're not sure about the truth of an article, dig deeper. Do a web search on the headline. Does it appear on other, more mainstream news outlets? You can also research the author. What other articles have they written? Do they all take alarming or controversial stances? Does the author often write satire? Possibly, the article itself is a joke—don't be the one to fall for it!

THE *ONION*

A former newspaper and now a website, the *Onion* is entirely satire. Its writers create news stories and headlines that sound realistic and official, but they're all made up to be funny. The articles often poke fun at news stories and people. They make outrageous claims that are designed for laughs. One 1999 story from the *Onion* jokingly said that scientists had discovered a race of skeleton people based on bones they had dug up.

Satire can be funny, but it can also be dangerous. Because it looks real and seems professionally done, many people who see it out of context fall for it. Keep that in mind the next time an article seems a bit too hilarious to be true.

Several sources online find and disprove disinformation. Sites such as Snopes.com and FactCheck.org often do all the research for you. They can usually identify where fake news comes from and provide context to help you better understand the issue. They may include links to more detailed information, or they might include interviews with experts who can explain what is true and what is false.

Combating Disinformation

You've clicked on an article. After reading it, you've done your research and found that it's not true. It's disinformation. It's harmful fake news, and you want to fight back. What can you do?

Your first task is to not click on any more links related to that one. If it's clickbait, you're just rewarding the site by giving it more views and more ad revenue. If you found the fake news on social media or in a news feed, check for a feedback option. Often, sites have buttons or menus that allow you to report news as fake. It's hard to say how much good it will do, but it only takes a few seconds.

Next, don't be part of the problem. Many users on social media are quick to share everything interesting they read, regardless of how true it is. They quickly hit the share or repost button without bothering to investigate. Resist the urge to do that. Always research anything you plan to share on social media. Make sure that anything that comes across your profile is real and true.

You can help stop the spread of disinformation on social media.

If you have friends, family, or followers who have shared a fake story, you can try posting in the comments section. This can be tricky. Some people will feel attacked if you call out their information as false. A comment can quickly turn into an argument. Go in with a polite comment. You could say something like, "I did a little research, and it turns out this isn't true." Then, if you have one, post a link to show your research.

Many people will respond well to that. They may take down the post and help prevent others from seeing it. Of course, that won't always be the case. They may argue back, they may get angry, or they may insult you. If that happens, nothing you say is likely to change their mind. It's time to back off. You took your best shot.

If someone seems interested in hearing what you have to say, it may be worth continuing the conversation. Just remember, you're there to be helpful. Accusing people or making them feel stupid won't do that. Be a resource for them. With some gentle guidance, you can help them become a bit more willing and able to research the stories that they share.

Being kind in online comments can help educate others on the importance of not spreading disinformation.

The Future of Disinformation

Disinformation isn't new. From the printing press to the internet, technology has helped spread both real and fake news. As technology continues to advance, the problem of disinformation is sure to get bigger.

One growing problem is government-sponsored fake news. Several foreign countries, including Russia, have been accused of creating and distributing false stories surrounding the US elections in 2016, 2020, and 2024. The stories aren't just about supporting one side or the other. They seem designed to create division among Americans. The creation of fake news on such large and organized scales is very tough to combat.

Technology has also played a part in the recent wave of disinformation. AI has boomed in the 2020s. AI can do amazing things. It has helped research new materials to improve the life and safety of batteries. It has helped scientists improve weather forecasting and warn of dangerous storms. It can even carry on conversations that make it seem human.

Even though AI can do many great and helpful things, it comes with a dark side. People can use it to create fake news articles. AI does a great job of making these articles look and feel like real news. It can also add fake images to stories to give them a bigger sense of credibility.

It doesn't stop with news stories either. High-powered AI can create lifelike images and videos called deepfakes. Deepfakes can show anyone doing just about anything.

Martí Batres at a press conference in 2024

AI can even fake a person's voice and their way of speaking. That's what happened in Mexico in 2024. A deepfake video showed Martí Batres, a prominent politician in Mexico, supporting a candidate for mayor. But he didn't do it. The video was created with AI. The quality of deepfakes can be so high that it's almost impossible to know what's true. You can't believe your eyes or your ears.

Yvette Clarke speaks at the US Capitol in 2024.

"It's important that we keep up with the technology," said US representative Yvette Clarke. "We've got to set up some guardrails. People can be deceived, and it only takes a split second. People are busy with their lives and they don't have the time to check every piece of information. AI being weaponized, in a political season, it could be extremely disruptive."

Sometimes, it seems as if disinformation just gets worse and worse. But it's not all bad news. Social media sites are adding tools to combat it. They've changed how news can be posted and offer ways to report fake stories. Meanwhile, many people are becoming more aware of the problem. According to one study, about 44 percent

SPOTTING DEEPFAKES

AI has grown by leaps and bounds in recent years. Modern AI can create lifelike images and videos that show just about anything. Experts have a few tricks that can help you spot deepfakes. They're not foolproof, but they can help.

- **Look at the hands. Some AI struggle to create realistic, lifelike human hands. If the hands look off, it's probably a fake image.**
- **Pay attention to objects in the background. Do they seem as if they belong? Are they placed in a natural way? Are they blurry for no reason?**
- **Look for writing on signs or buildings. Does it make sense? Do the letters and symbols look right?**
- **Check the faces. Do they look overly smooth or artistic? Are they too perfect? If so, that could suggest it's a deepfake.**

of Americans clicked on a fake news article during the 2016 US presidential election. By the 2020 election, that number was down to about 26 percent.

Meanwhile, AI can also be a tool to fight disinformation. AI can often identify fake news and help sites take steps to delete it. It can't do it alone, though. Fake news only thrives when people believe it. The best defense against it is to think critically and do your research.

Important Dates

mid-1400s German inventor Johannes Gutenberg introduces the printing press.

1475 A false story spreads that a Jewish community in Trent, Italy, captured and killed a young boy. Fifteen people are wrongly killed as punishment.

1934 Colonel Robert Wilson claims to have snapped a photo of the Loch Ness Monster. Years later, the photo is revealed as fake.

1983 The modern internet is born.

1991 The World Wide Web is introduced.

2004 Myspace becomes the first social media site with more than one million users.

2012 Hurricane Sandy batters the East Coast of North America. Disinformation online makes finding real news about the disaster difficult.

2016 Foreign countries flood social media with fake stories designed to divide Americans during the presidential election.

2017	A fake story tricks people into believing that Reese's Peanut Butter Cups are made with toxic ingredients.
2020	Joe Biden defeats Donald Trump in a close presidential race. Trump spreads disinformation, insisting that he had been cheated.
	Disinformation about the disease COVID-19 creates confusion and distrust.
2021	After disinformation about the 2020 US presidential election spreads online, Trump supporters stage an attack on the US Capitol.
	A fake article claims that solar panels are causing global climate change.
2023	The REAL Political Advertisements Act, a law that would limit how AI-generated material can be used in political advertisements, is introduced in Congress.
2024	Disinformation spreads during elections.

Source Notes

9 Alex Kasprak, "Three Reasons You Should Stop Eating Peanut Butter Cups," Snopes.com, March 31, 2017, https://www.snopes.com/fact-check/peanut-butter-cups/.

16 Tom Huddleston Jr., "In 1995, Bill Gates Made These Predictions About Streaming Movies and Fake News on the Internet," CNBC.com, May 31, 2019, https://www.cnbc.com/2019/05/31/bill-gates-1995-predictions-about-streaming-movies-fake-news.html.

24 Lauren Egan, "'We Won': Trump Spreads Misinformation About 2020 Election During Final Georgia Rally," NBC News, January 4, 2021, https://www.nbcnews.com/politics/2020-election/we-won-trump-spreads-misinformation-about-2020-election-during-final-n1252802.

24 "Disarming Disinformation: Our Shared Responsibility," US Department of State, February 8, 2024, https://www.state.gov/disarming-disinformation/.

29 Matt Brown, "Fact Check: Could Taking Vitamin C Cure—or Prevent—COVID-19?," *USA Today*, March 24, 2020, https://www.usatoday.com/story/news/factcheck/2020/03/24/coronavirus-fact-check-could-vitamin-c-cure-covid-19/2904303001/.

40 David Klepper, "AI-Generated Disinformation Poses Threat of Misleading Voters in 2024 Election," PBS, May 14, 2023, https://www.pbs.org/newshour/politics/ai-generated-disinformation-poses-threat-of-misleading-voters-in-2024-election.

Selected Bibliography

Barclay, Donald A. *Disinformation: The Nature of Facts and Lies in the Post-Truth Era*. Lanham, MD: Rowman & Littlefield, 2021.

De Witte, Melissa. "What Stanford Research Reveals About Disinformation and How to Address It." Stanford Report, April 13, 2022. https://news.stanford.edu/stories/2022/04/know-disinformation-address.

"Disarming Disinformation: Our Shared Responsibility." US Department of State, February 8, 2024. https://www.state.gov/disarming-disinformation.

Gerbina, T. V. "Science Disinformation: On the Problem of Fake News." *Scientific and Technical Information Processing* 48 (February 2022): 290–298. https://doi.org/10.3103/S0147688221040092.

Gregory, Josh. *The Trouble with Deepfakes*. Ann Arbor, MI: Cherry Lake, 2024.

Rissman, Rebecca. *Loch Ness Uncovered: How Fake News Fueled the Greatest Monster Hoax of All Time*. New York: Astra Young Readers, 2024.

Learn More

FactCheck.org
https://www.factcheck.org

Gravel, Elise. *Killer Underwear Invasion! How to Spot Fake News, Disinformation and Conspiracy Theories.* San Francisco: Chronicle Books, 2022.

Hudak, Heather C. *Misinformation, Disinformation, and Censorship.* New York: Crabtree, 2024.

Idzikowski, Lisa. *The Challenges of AI.* Minneapolis: Lerner Publications, 2025.

National Geographic Kids: Spotting Fake News
https://kids.nationalgeographic.com/magazine/article/fake-news

NSPCC: Fake News, Hoaxes and Misinformation
https://www.nspcc.org.uk/keeping-children-safe/online-safety/inappropriate-explicit-content/fake-news/

Index

Photo Acknowledgments

Image credits: KristenLynnWolfePhoto/Shutterstock, p. 6; fizkes/Getty Images, p. 8; Matteo Zerbini/500px/Getty Images, p. 11; Keystone/Getty Images, p. 12; Universal Images Group/Getty Images, p. 13; Library of Congress, p. 14; Mickey Adair/Getty Images, p. 15; Michel GANGN/AFP via Getty Images, p. 17; Juana Arias/The Washington Post via Getty Images, p. 18; Mario Tama/Getty Images, p. 19; NICHOLAS KAMM/AFP via Getty Images, p. 20; Drew Angerer/Getty Images, p. 22; Morry Gash/AP/Bloomberg via Getty Images, p. 23; Eric Lee/Bloomberg via Getty Images, p. 25; Bill Clark/CQ-Roll Call, Inc via Getty Images, p. 26; Aydin Palabiyikoglu/Getty Images, p. 28; Sergey Uryadnikov/Alamy, p. 30; FG Trade/Getty Images, p. 32; True Images/Alamy, p. 34; Mehaniq/Shutterstock, p. 36; MoMo Productions/Getty Images, p. 37; IMAGO/Alejandro Medina Guzman/Eyepix/Alamy, p. 39; AP Photo/J. Scott Applewhite, p. 40. Design elements: Golubovy/Shutterstock; Rudchenko Liliia/Shutterstock; Here/Shutterstock; doa bunda/Shutterstock; RoseRodionova/Shutterstock; mejorana/Shutterstock.

Cover images: ymgerman/Shutterstock; The7Dew/Shutterstock; Lucky Team Studio/Shutterstock.